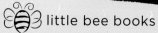

little bee books

New York, NY
Text copyright © 2019 by Alice B. McGinty
Illustrations copyright © 2019 by Tomoko Suzuki

For more information about special discounts on bulk purchases,
please contact Little Bee Books at sales@littlebeebooks.com.
Manufactured in China RRD 1122
First Edition
6 8 10 9 7 5

Library of Congress Cataloging-in-Publication Data
Names: McGinty, Alice B., 1963– author. | Suzuki, Tomoko, illustrator.
Title: Pancakes to parathas: breakfast around the world / by Alice B.
McGinty; illustrated by Tomoko Suzuki. | Description: First edition.
New York, New York: Little Bee Books, an imprint of Bonnier Publishing, USA, 2019.
Audience: Age 4–8. | Audience: Grade K to grade 3. | Includes bibliographical references.
Identifiers: LCCN 2018013320 | Subjects: LCSH: Breakfasts—Juvenile literature.
Pancakes, waffles, etc.—Juvenile literature. | LCGFT: Cookbooks.
Classification: LCC TX733.M475 2019 | DDC 641.81/53—dc23
LC record available at https://lccn.loc.gov/2018013320
ISBN 978-1-4998-0712-7

littlebeebooks.com

Pancakes to Parathas

— Breakfast Around the World —

by Alice B. McGinty   **illustrated by** Tomoko Suzuki

little bee books

Acknowledgments

I'd like to thank these friends from each country who provided the details that brought this book to life: Christopher Cheng and Bini Szacsvay in Australia; my son, Jake McGinty, who lived in Japan; Olivia Han and Joy Ding from China; Sharmar Kishan from India (owner of the Bombay Indian Grill in Champaign, Illinois); Miri Leshem-Pelly in Israel; Charles Briggs from Nigeria; Mina Witteman in the Netherlands; Keely Parrack and Louise Cliffe-Minns from England; Andrea Aguiar from Brazil; Eva Davis from Pressa One Love Restaurant in Negril, Jamaica; and Terrill Martinez in Mexico.

To my agent, Steven Chudney, who planted the seed, and to the generous people from around the globe who helped it grow by sharing information, stories, and scrumptious food
— **ABM**

For Chisato
— **TS**

It's breakfast time around the world,
in countries near and far.
Wake up, world! It's time to eat,
no matter where you are!

What's for breakfast in . . . Australia?

Breakfast in Australia
is a black and salty paste.
Thinly spread on toasted bread . . .
it's quite a shocking taste!

Australia

VEGEMITE

Vegemite (VEJ-eh-mite) is the name of this salty paste. It's made from brewer's yeast—an ingredient in bread-making—and it's loaded with vitamins. It may take time to get used to the strong taste, but kids in Australia love it. They spread it on bread for breakfast, and they like it so much that they bring Vegemite sandwiches with tomato or cheese for school lunch. They also spread Vegemite between crackers and squeeze, so the spread comes out of the cracker holes like little worms!

Wake up, countries,
one by one.
Eat breakfast with
the rising sun!

What's for breakfast in . . . Japan?

When kids wake up in Tokyo,
their breakfast may be slimy,
soured soybeans, fish and rice,
and one raw egg. "Just try me!"

Japan

Natto (NAH-tow), or soured soybeans, has a sour taste and slimy texture, but it is part of a nutritious, traditional Japanese breakfast. Breakfast in Japan also includes cooked fish and rice, which kids may mix in bowls with soy sauce and natto, topped with a raw egg. This hearty breakfast prepares children for school. As kids walk to school in Tokyo, they wear bright yellow caps so they can easily be seen by drivers on the busy streets.

Now, cross a little
patch of sea
to find a different
cup of tea.

What's for breakfast in . . . China?

Shanghai's breakfast is a ball,
sold on crowded streets.
Packed round and tight with sticky rice,
it's filled with juicy meat.

China

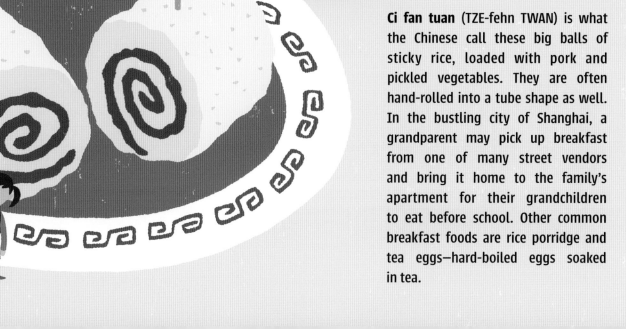

Ci fan tuan (TZE-fehn TWAN) is what the Chinese call these big balls of sticky rice, loaded with pork and pickled vegetables. They are often hand-rolled into a tube shape as well. In the bustling city of Shanghai, a grandparent may pick up breakfast from one of many street vendors and bring it home to the family's apartment for their grandchildren to eat before school. Other common breakfast foods are rice porridge and tea eggs—hard-boiled eggs soaked in tea.

Follow the sun
from east to west.
Where is sunrise
coming next?

What's for breakfast in . . . India?

Moms in northern India
make bread, fried flat and round.
Rip some off, then dip in sauce.
The spices will astound!

India

Paratha (pah-RAH-ta) is fried, round flatbread made with layered dough and it is sometimes stuffed with spicy mashed potatoes. Families gather at their table to eat pie-shaped slices of paratha. They rip off pieces of the hot bread and dip it into sauces for flavor. Sauces can include a mildly spiced yogurt or chutney. Chutney is a relish that comes in flavors like mango or tomato and is often combined with hot peppers and spices such as ginger or cilantro.

Gather round!
The family's here . . .
a kitchen full
of breakfast cheer.

What's for breakfast in . . . Israel?

Breakfast here in Israel
is a giant homegrown spread.
Choose some olives from the grove.
Have some salad. Pass the bread!

Israel

Israeli breakfasts are famous for being feasts filled with fresh foods grown in the warm climate. Busy families may eat quickly on weekday mornings, but on Saturdays, the Sabbath, they relax together at breakfast, passing around foods from the big spread on the table. Kids eat chopped salads made from tomatoes, cucumbers, and onions. They eat breads, such as pita and braided challah, along with cottage cheese, eggs, and salted herring. Since the Israeli people originated from many countries, Israeli foods come from all over. They include burekas, a filled pastry from Turkey, and shakshuka, an egg-topped tomato mixture from North Africa.

The day's first food
is such a treat.
Now, who's awake
and wants to eat?

What's for breakfast in . . . Nigeria?

In Africa's Nigeria,
a kid's first meal is crunchy,
deep-fried fritters made of beans,
cooked with peppers—hot and munchy!

Akara (ah-KAH-rah) is the name of these crunchy fritters that Nigerian families eat. They are made with flour ground from black-eyed peas, which are a type of bean, and they are cooked with hot peppers, such as chilis, to add flavor. Kids from villages and towns carry their akara wrapped in a brown paper bag and eat them as they walk to school each morning.

While one place sleeps,
another plays.
But always, breakfast
starts their days.

**What's for breakfast in . . .
the Netherlands?**

Delicious chocolate sprinkles,
spread on buttered bread.
It's the perfect morning meal
to coax you out of bed!

Netherlands

Hagelslag (HAH-chl-slahch) is the name of these flavorful sprinkles that children and adults spread onto thick slices of buttered bread. They can choose chocolate, vanilla, or a colorful mix of fruit-flavored hagelslag before they head off to school. In the city of Amsterdam, most kids bike to school, with younger kids riding on the front or the back of a parent's bike.

Who's next to hear
alarm bells chime,
telling them it's
wake-up time?

**What's for breakfast in . . .
the United Kingdom?**

A morning treat in London
has sausages and bacon—
a hearty English breakfast
to warm you when you waken.

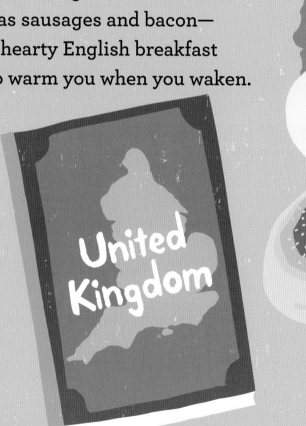

United
Kingdom

Rashers (RASH-ahs) are thick slices of bacon, and bangers are sausages. They're part of a full English breakfast, a plate piled with baked beans, toast fried in butter, fried mushrooms and tomatoes, and a fried egg on top. This breakfast is a treat on weekends or holidays. On weekdays, kids may eat cereal, such as Weetabix, which is served hot or cold with milk and sugar. Or they might have eggs and soldiers—soft-boiled eggs served in egg cups with sticks of toast to dip into the yolk.

Now head south.
Cross oceans grand.
You'll end up
in a different land.

What's for breakfast in . . . Brazil?

Kids drink coffee, warm and sweet,
for breakfast in Brazil!
It's smooth as silk, with lots of milk.
Sip, then dip, then fill!

Brazil

Café de manhã (KAH-fey deh MAN-yah) is what Brazilians call breakfast, and it means "morning coffee." Children's morning coffee, called café con leche (coffee with milk), has more milk than coffee and is sweetened with sugar. To complete this light breakfast, many children love fruit and a fresh mini baguette, baked that morning at a neighborhood bakery, to dip in their coffee.

Across the waves
the sun is rising.
An island's time
for energizing.

What's for breakfast in . . . Jamaica?

Breakfast in Jamaica
is yellow like the sun.
Cornmeal porridge, thick and sweet.
Come and get it, everyone!

Jamaica

Cornmeal porridge is often cooked with coconut milk, sugar, vanilla, and cinnamon to give it a full, sweet flavor. As Jamaican kids start the day, dressed neatly in their school uniforms, they may also eat tasty yellow fruits such as papaya, boiled yam, pumpkin, and fried plantains, which are a fruit like bananas. Some might like **ackee** (AH-key), Jamaica's national fruit, cooked with saltfish, which is a dried, salted fish. Cooked together, ackee and saltfish look like scrambled eggs—another part of a yellow Jamaican breakfast.

As Earth keeps turning,
chase the sun.
Its westward trip
is almost done.

What's for breakfast in . . . Mexico?

Top a corn tortilla
with salsa, eggs, and beans,
for a spicy, feisty breakfast
of yellows, reds, and greens.

Mexico

Huevos (HWAY-vos) is the Spanish word for eggs. In Mexican families, huevos are served with many colorful and tasty ingredients, including beans, cheese, peppers, and guacamole, and are topped with either salsa roja (red salsa) or salsa verde (green salsa). Life and colors abound in a Mexican kitchen, with large extended families all gathered around colorful tablecloths and baskets of warm tortillas, as joyful music plays on the radio.

Breakfast to breakfast,
you've come a LONG way!
There's one more breakfast left . . .
in the U. S. of A.

What's for breakfast in . . .
the United States of America?

Is it pancakes? Maybe cereal?
Or bacon, eggs, and ham?
A big tall glass of orange juice,
served with toast and jam?

U.S.A.

On busy school days, breakfast for kids in the United States often consists of cereal or a bagel or toast and jam with a glass of orange juice and some milk. When families have time for a bigger breakfast, moms and dads may cook eggs with bacon or ham. They might make waffles, or, if kids are lucky, pancakes cooked with blueberries or chocolate chips. Some parents even make pancakes in special shapes.

From pancakes to parathas,
from Vegemite to toast,
wake up, world, it's time to eat
the meal we love the most!

United Kingdom

U.S.A.

Mexico

Jamaica

Netherlands

Nigeria

Brazil

Breakfast Around the World

Israel

China

Japan

India

Australia